BOOK B

Early Reading Comprehension

in Varied Subject Matter

JANE ERVIN

SOCIAL STUDIES

SCIENCE MATHEMATICS

LOGICAL THINKING

THE ARTS

LITERATURE

GENERAL TOPICS

EDUCATORS PUBLISHING SERVICE
Cambridge and Toronto

Dr. Jane Ervin works in Washington, D.C. with children with reading and learning problems and advises parents on educational needs. Her advice is sought by schools, government, and educational and parent organizations throughout the country. Dr. Ervin has been principal of a school, taught children of all ages, and trained teachers in reading and basic skills. She received her doctorate in education and post-doctorate diploma in English from UCLA.

Dr. Ervin would like to thank the National Geographic Society for their interest in the development of these books, and particularly the editors of *World* magazine, whose lively, interesting articles provided a stimulating resource that contributed greatly to the quality of the selections.

Illustrator: George Phillips

Printed in USA

ISBN 978-0-8388-0622-7

9 10 11 PPG 12 11 10

CONTENTS

subject: general topics

subject: social studies

subject: science

subject: logical thinking

subject: math

subject: literature

subject: the arts

1 Camels

What's in a camel's **hump**?

Camels can **gulp** down about twenty-five gallons of water in just ten minutes — and not need another drink for a week! They can do this because they can **store** water in little bags in their stomachs and in other parts of their bodies.

Camels do not store water in their humps, as people often think. The hump is where they store food, in the form of fat.*

Camels are just right for **desert** travel because they can store food and water. They are very strong and can carry heavy **loads**. They don't sink into the sand. They also have long eyelashes that stop the sand from getting into their eyes.

The passage is about

(a) what camels are like

(b) how to look after a camel

(c) a trip across the desert

*See how the camel got its hump in the story on page 51.

1

Can you remember?

1. How long does it take a camel to drink twenty-five gallons of water?
   - (a) one minute
   - ((b)) ten minutes
   - (c) one hour

2. How long will this drink last the camel?
   - (a) one day
   - ((b)) one week
   - (c) one month

3. What do camels store in their humps?
   - ((a)) food
   - (b) water
   - (c) air

4. Camels are
   - ((a)) strong
   - (b) weak
   - (c) small

5. Camels are good desert animals because they have
   - (a) long necks
   - (b) long legs
   - ((c)) long eyelashes

Put the sentences in the correct order.

__2__ Water is not stored in the camels' humps.

__3__ Camels are good for desert travel.

__4__ They are also very strong and can carry heavy loads.

__1__ Camels can gulp down about twenty-five gallons of water in just ten minutes.

Match the words with their meanings.

__a__ 1. hump   (a) lump, something that sticks up

__d__ 2. gulp   (b) heavy things that are carried

__c__ 3. desert   (c) dry, sandy place that goes on for miles

__e__ 4. store   (d) swallow quickly

__b__ 5. loads   (e) to keep or put away, to use at a later time

Write about it.

1. Write two sentences about the same subject (write about a different subject from the selection). Use one of the words from "Match the words with their meanings."

2. Imagine that you have to go on a week-long trip across the desert, as camels often do. How would you carry the food and water you will need? What kind of food would you bring with you?

2   The Pony Express

What was the Pony Express?

Do you think being a mail carrier is **dangerous** and **daring**? Well, it was in the early days when there were no airplanes or trains to carry the mail.

In the 1860s — over a hundred years ago — the mail was taken out West by the Pony Express. Daring, brave riders sped across the country on horseback, riding day and night. They had to ride through lonely, dangerous places and face all kinds of weather. Sometimes they were attacked by people or animals, or by robbers who wanted to steal the mail.

Stations were set up along the **route**. There a rider could quickly change to a new horse. Sometimes a new rider and horse took over. There was never a moment's **delay**. As soon as the change had been made the mail was on its way again.

The passage is about

   (a) a horse race   (b) delivering the mail   (c) robbers

Can you remember?

1. The Pony Express took mail to
   (a) the South   (b) the West   (c) the North

2. The riders rode
   (a) without stopping   (b) taking some rests   (c) only during the day

3. The riders carried guns
   (a) all the time   (b) only in dangerous   (c) it doesn't say
                              places

4. What do you think robbers wanted in the mail?
   (a) gold   (b) jewels   (c) money or legal
                                                     papers

5. The riders tried to
   (a) go as fast   (b) carry heavy   (c) make a lot of
       as they could   loads   money

Put the sentences in the correct order.

_____ The mail was on its way again.

_____ There were no airplanes or trains to carry the mail.

_____ There were stations set up along the route.

_____ Daring and brave riders rode quickly across the country.

Match the words with their meanings.

_____ 1. dangerous   (a) places to stop

_____ 2. daring   (b) not safe

_____ 3. stations   (c) brave

_____ 4. route   (d) wait, put off

_____ 5. delay   (e) the path one follows

Write about it.

1. Write two sentences about the same subject (write about a different subject from the selection). Use one of the words from "Match the words with their meanings."

2. Write and mail a letter to a friend or relative. It will arrive a little faster than in the 1860s! Tell this person what you did over the weekend, or tell some other news about your life.

3 The Money Maker

How does Jane's father make money?

Jane's father makes dollar bills. He works for the government in Washington, D.C. and is called an **engraver** (en-GRAY-ver). It took him many years to learn his job.

He makes pictures on a **steel plate** by cutting thin lines into the plate with a very sharp tool. Other people work on the plates with him. For example, he does the faces while someone else does the letters.

When the plates are finished, they are put into a printing **press**. The plates are then covered with ink and pressed against large sheets of paper. This prints the pictures onto the paper.

The large sheets with many dollar bills printed on them are then cut up into single dollar bills.

The passage is about

   (a) steel   (b) paper   (c) money

Can you remember?

1. Jane's father is
   (a) a painter   (b) an engraver   (c) a toolmaker

2. He makes pictures on
   (a) steel   (b) paper   (c) wood

3. He uses
   (a) pencil   (b) a paint brush   (c) a sharp tool

4. The thing he cuts lines into is called
   (a) a plate   (b) a cup   (c) a sheet

5. The finished plates are put into
   (a) a cupboard   (b) an ink machine   (c) a printing press

Put the sentences in the correct order.

_____ Ink is put on the plates.

_____ Jane's dad does the faces.

_____ It took him many years to learn his job.

_____ Jane's father makes dollar bills.

Match the words with their meanings.

_____ 1. press   (a) someone who carves pictures onto steel plates

_____ 2. steel   (b) a smooth, flat piece of metal

_____ 3. plate   (c) a hard, tough metal

_____ 4. engraver   (d) a machine that prints

Write about it.

1. Write two sentences about the same subject (write about a different subject from the selection). Use one of the words from "Match the words with their meanings."

2. Draw a new design for our five-dollar bill that Jane's father could engrave. Then write why the things in your drawing are important.

4 Mustangs

What is a mustang?

Horses have played a very **important** part in American history. But there were no horses in this country until the Spanish brought them here about 400 years ago. These horses came to be called mustangs.

Native Americans found the mustangs in the western part of the country. They had run away from their owners and were **roaming** free. They had become tough and strong living in the **wilderness**, and were very fast. They were about the size of a pony and were very beautiful with their long, **flowing** manes and tails.

Native Americans looked after the mustangs well. They rode them to hunt, to get around, and just to enjoy the ride.

There are still **herds** of wild mustangs roaming free. Some are rounded up each year. They are then sold to be trained for some lucky person to ride.

The passage is about

   (a) cars   (b) horses   (c) food

Can you remember?

1. Who brought the mustangs to this country?

   (a) the English (b) the Spanish (c) the French

2. In what part of the U.S. did Native Americans find the mustangs?

   (a) southern (b) eastern (c) western

3. What made the mustangs strong and tough?

   (a) living in the wilderness (b) eating a lot (c) carrying heavy loads

4. Mustangs are *not*

   (a) fast (b) beautiful (c) large

5. Which is correct?

   (a) There are no wild mustangs. (b) Wild mustangs are caught every year. (c) Mustangs cannot be trained.

Put the sentences in the correct order.

_____ Native Americans took care of the mustangs.

_____ They had run away and were roaming free.

_____ Horses have played a very important part in our history.

_____ They are then sold to be trained for some lucky person to ride.

Match the words with their meanings.

_____ 1. herds (a) going from place to place

_____ 2. roaming (b) groups of animals

_____ 3. wilderness (c) of great value

_____ 4. flowing (d) hanging loose and waving

_____ 5. important (e) a wild place with no one living in it

10

Write about it.

1. Write two sentences about the same subject (write about a different subject from the selection). Use one of the words from "Match the words with their meanings."

2. Some people object to selling wild mustangs. Give reasons for and against rounding up and selling these wild horses.

5 Our First Money

What kind of money did the first **settlers** use?

There were no dollar bills or coins in the early days of our country. What did the settlers use for money?

At first they **copied** the Native Americans and used wampum. Wampum was made of seashells. The shells were broken into pieces with stone tools. The pieces were then rubbed until they were smooth and **shiny**. Dark shells were worth more because there weren't many of them.

Things that were **scarce** and much needed in those days were also used as money. For example, the early settlers used tea, sugar, horses, and **gunpowder** for money.

The passage is about

   (a) how to find shells   (b) how to make tea   (c) our first money

Can you remember?

1. In the early days of our country, people did not have

   (a) coins   (b) sugar   (c) tea

2. Wampum was made from

    (a) sugar   (b) shells   (c) gunpowder

3. The tools used to break the shells were made of

    (a) stone   (b) wood   (c) steel

4. Dark shells were worth more because

    (a) they were   (b) there were more   (c) there weren't

         prettier   of them   many of them

5. What was also used as money

    (a) beaver's teeth   (b) salt   (c) horses

Put the sentences in the correct order.

_____ Dark shells were worth more.

_____ What did the settlers use for money?

_____ The early settlers used tea, sugar, horses, and gunpowder for money.

_____ At first the settlers copied the Native Americans.

Match the words with their meanings.

_____ 1. settlers   (a) bright

_____ 2. copied   (b) people who move to a new land

_____ 3. shiny   (c) did the same as

_____ 4. scarce   (d) exploding powder used in guns

_____ 5. gunpowder   (e) hard to find; not very much of

Write about it.

1. Write two sentences about the same subject (write about a different subject from the selection). Use one of the words from "Match the words with their meanings."

2. What would you pick to use as money if we had no dollar bills or coins? Explain the reason for your choice.

13

6 John Glenn

Who is John Glenn?

He was elected a **senator** and went to Washington, D.C. As a senator, he worked on the laws of our country.

But it was not always that way. Before John Glenn was working with problems of this world, he was dealing with outer space. In February 1962, he became the first American to travel in the earth's orbit.

He had always wanted to be an **astronaut**. So you know how **thrilled** he must have been when he heard the countdown: ". . . five, four, three, two, one, blast off!" His space ship was called Friendship 7. He went around the earth three times before landing **gently** in the sea.

In October 1998 Glenn got to return to space as part of the crew of the space shuttle *Discovery*.

The passage is about the first American person

    (a) to go into   (b) to travel in   (c) to land on

        outer space   the earth's orbit   the moon

Can you remember?

1. John Glenn became
   (a) an airline pilot
   (b) a senator
   (c) a scientist

2. When did he first go around the earth?
   (a) 1962
   (b) 1972
   (c) 1982

3. How many times did he go around the earth in 1962?
   (a) one
   (b) two
   (c) three

4. His space ship was called
   (a) Friendship
   (b) Happiness
   (c) Lucky

5. Where did he land?
   (a) in a field
   (b) in the desert
   (c) in the sea

Put the sentences in the correct order.

_____ But it was not always that way.

_____ He worked on our country's laws.

_____ ". . . five, four, three, two, one, blast off!"

_____ He flew around the earth three times.

Match the words with their meanings.

_____ 1. gently   (a) very excited, happy

_____ 2. senator   (b) a person people vote for to make laws in
                              Washington; each state chooses two
_____ 3. astronaut   senators

_____ 4. thrilled   (c) someone who goes into outer space in a
                              spaceship

                          (d) easily, softly

Write about it.

1. Write two sentences about the same subject (write about a different subject from the selection). Use one of the words from "Match the words with their meanings."

2. Would you like to become an astronaut and travel in outer space? Tell why or why not.

15

7   Money in Other Places

What do the people who live in the South Pacific **islands** use for money?

In the early days of this country we used shells for money.* Some people who live in the Solomon (SOL-o-mon) Islands in the Pacific Ocean still do. They put the shells on strings and wear them around their necks. They use paper money, too. But sometimes important things like land, a **canoe**, or a **bride** are paid for with shells.

Yap is an island in the Pacific Ocean. The money that the people of Yap have is very big. Some of the money can be ten feet tall — much taller than people. This money is made from stones. It is so big and heavy that people in Yap keep it in front of their houses or in a bank in the village.

Many of the stones have holes **drilled** through them. When people want to move their money, they put a big **pole** through the hole in the middle of the stone so they can carry it.

*See the story on page 12.

16

The passage is about

    (a) how to make money   (b) why you should keep shells and stones   (c) what other people use for money

Can you remember?

1. The people of the Solomon Islands keep their money

    (a) in boxes   (b) in front of their homes   (c) around their necks

2. What do the Solomon Islands people use for money?

    (a) shells   (b) stones   (c) canoes

3. What do the people of Yap use for money?

    (a) shells   (b) stones   (c) poles

4. Yap money

    (a) has a hole in it   (b) shines   (c) is very small

5. The people of Yap carry their money

    (a) in boxes   (b) on their heads   (c) on poles

Put the sentences in the correct order.

_____ They put the shells on strings.

_____ They also use paper money.

_____ Many of the stones have holes in them.

_____ The people of Yap have money that is very big.

Match the words with their meanings.

_____ 1. islands   (a) a long, thin piece of wood or metal

_____ 2. pole   (b) made a hole in something

_____ 3. bride   (c) lands that have water all around them

_____ 4. drilled   (d) a small, light, narrow boat moved by paddles

_____ 5. canoe   (e) woman who has just been married

Write about it.

1. Write two sentences about the same subject (write about a different subject from the selection). Use one of the words from "Match the words with their meanings."

2. Think of some things that might make a stone valuable, such as color, size, shape, and how rare it is, and list them. Then decide which of these things are most important to you. Put the list in order from most important to least important.

8 What Am I?

I come in tiny little bits. What am I?

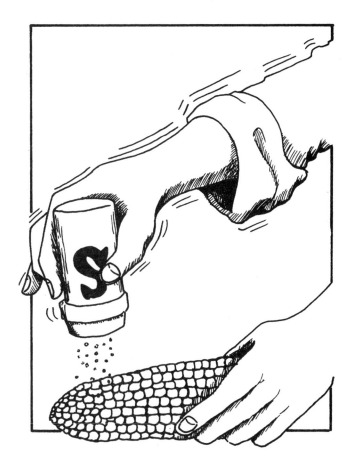

Long ago I was needed in food to keep it from **spoiling**. Today I am still used to keep meat like ham and bacon **fresh**.

Sometimes I have no color and sometimes I am white. I come in tiny bits like sand. When I'm in water you can't see me at all. And I'm found in water a lot.

Your body can't do without me. But too much of me is not good for you.

You never eat me alone. But you use me a lot in cooking and often sprinkle me on your food because I make it taste better. But, **beware**! If you have too much of me you'll be thirsty.

One more **tip** — I can melt snow, but I can also be used to **freeze** ice cream.

What am I?

The passage is about

    (a) sand   (b) sugar   (c) salt

Can you remember?

1. It's
   - (a) good to eat alone
   - (b) not good to eat
   - (c) good with other food

2. Long ago it was used to
   - (a) keep food from going bad
   - (b) keep the water fresh
   - (c) stop people from getting sick

3. What color is it?
   - (a) brown
   - (b) yellow
   - (c) It can have no color

4. It can melt
   - (a) ice cream
   - (b) snow
   - (c) sugar

5. Your body
   - (a) doesn't need it
   - (b) needs some, but not too much
   - (c) needs a lot of it

Put the sentences in the correct order.

_____ Your body can't do without me.

_____ I can make snow melt.

_____ You never eat me by myself.

_____ I have no color.

Match the words with their meanings.

_____ 1. fresh   (a) make into ice

_____ 2. spoiling   (b) like new

_____ 3. beware   (c) hint

_____ 4. tip   (d) be careful; watch out

_____ 5. freeze   (e) becoming bad; not fresh

Write about it.

1. Write two sentences about the same subject (write about a different subject from the selection). Use one of the words from "Match the words with their meanings."

2. Write about something. Use lots of details, but do not say what it is. Then show the description to a friend. See if you have described it so well that your friend can guess what it is.

9 Meet Yourself

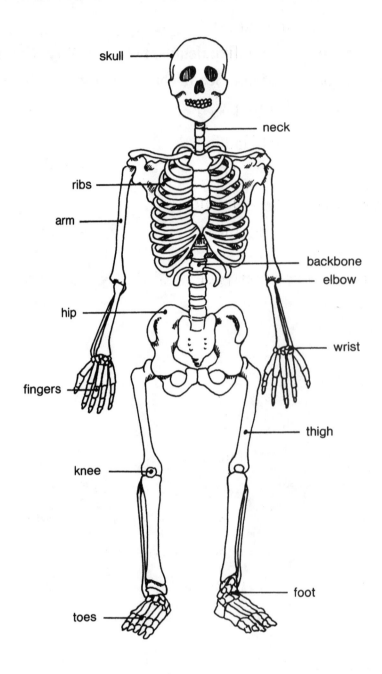

skull

neck

ribs

arm

backbone
elbow

hip

wrist

fingers

thigh

knee

foot

toes

Here's a picture of you. What is it called?

The chart is about

   (a) a ghost
   (b) a Halloween **costume**
   (c) the bones of your body

Can you remember?

1. The chart is called

   (a) an **outline**   (b) a **skeleton**   (c) a body

2. The longest bones are in your

   (a) legs   (b) fingers   (c) ankle

3. Your **skull** is your

   (a) hip bone   (b) knee bone   (c) head bone

4. The largest bones are *not* found in your

   (a) legs   (b) ribs   (c) toes

5. The smallest bones are *not* found in your

   (a) hips   (b) fingers   (c) toes

Put in the correct order from your head down to your toes.

_____ feet

_____ ribs

_____ hips

_____ neck

Match the words with their meanings.

_____ 1. outline   (a) a special kind of outfit to wear

_____ 2. skeleton   (b) the outside shape of something

_____ 3. skull   (c) the bones of your body

_____ 4. costume   (d) head bone

Write about it.

1. Write two sentences about the same subject (write about a different subject from the selection). Use one of the words from "Match the words with their meanings."

2. Some people think skeletons look scary. Write a scary story about a skeleton that comes to life.

10 How to Lose Weight

When do you weigh nothing?

When the first astronauts went into space,* an odd thing happened to them. They lost some weight. In fact they lost all their weight. They became so light they could **float** around in their space ship. They could stand on their hands, turn head-over-heels, or sit in the air.

It's fun to be **weightless** but it brings its problems. If you try to eat, your food floats off your spoon. If you read a book, it won't stay in your hands. If you try to walk, your feet won't stay on the ground.

All the food and other objects have to be kept in closed boxes that are **bolted down**. The astronauts' feet are kept down by rubber cups on the **soles** of their shoes, which stick to the floor.

Why do we float when we go into space? It's because we leave the pull of **gravity** that comes from the earth.

*See the story on page 14.

The passage is about

    (a) how to become smaller   (b) what happens when you go into space   (c) why we stand up on earth

Can you remember?

1. The astronauts lost

    (a) some weight   (b) no weight   (c) all of their weight

2. Which is correct?

    (a) everything floats in space   (b) only people float in space   (c) only light things float in space

3. The astronauts' feet are kept down by

    (a) hooks   (b) cups   (c) rocks

4. In order to become an astronaut, you must

    (a) not weigh much   (b) be able to fly   (c) It doesn't say.

5. The astronauts float in space because

    (a) they wear suits full of air   (b) they are put on a diet before going   (c) they leave the pull of gravity

Put the sentences in the correct order.

_____ All the food has to be kept in closed boxes.

_____ An odd thing happened to the first astronauts.

_____ It's fun to be weightless.

_____ Why do we float when we go into space?

Match the words with their meanings.

_____ 1. soles   (a) rise on top of something

_____ 2. weightless   (b) fastened tightly

_____ 3. float   (c) without weight

_____ 4. bolted down   (d) pull from the center of the earth

_____ 5. gravity   (e) the bottoms of shoes or feet

Write about it.

1. Write two sentences about the same subject (write about a different subject from the selection). Use one of the words from "Match the words with their meanings."

2. Being in a place with no gravity could be fun or difficult. Describe some things you like to do (such as playing basketball or e-mailing friends) and tell how a lack of gravity would affect these activities.

11   The "Bear" Facts

How did the grizzly bear get its name?

Bears can be black, brown, white, or any **shade** of these colors. I like the grizzly bear. It is brown, but the tips of its fur are silver. Grizzly means "Mixed with white hairs."

Bears are large — taller than humans, and some are as heavy as a small car. They are strong and fast — not something to bump into on a dark night! They are **fierce** fighters and have plenty of sharp teeth for chewing **flesh** and **grinding up** bones.

Bears find all sorts of things to eat — deer, rabbits, mice, fish, berries, nuts, plants, insects, and honey along with the bees.

Some people think bears are also smart. They sleep the winter away in their **dens**, living off their body fat.

This passage is about

    (a) meeting a bear on   (b) feeding bears   (c) what bears are like
         a dark night

Can you remember?

1. A grizzly bear

    (a) cries a lot   (b) has silver-tipped   (c) is black
                         fur

2. Bears can be as heavy as

    (a) a human   (b) an elephant   (c) a small car

3. Bears are

    (a) fast   (b) slow   (c) it doesn't say

4. Bears eat

    (a) only animals   (b) only plants   (c) almost anything

5. Where do bears get their food in the winter?

    (a) their own bodies   (b) the ground   (c) trees

Put the sentences in the correct order.

_____ Bears find all kinds of good things to eat.

_____ Bears are also smart.

_____ Bears can be black, brown, white, or any color in between.

_____ Bears are large.

Match the words with their meanings.

_____ 1. shade   (a) places for wild animals to live or rest

_____ 2. dens   (b) cruel, strong

_____ 3. fierce   (c) breaking into small bits

_____ 4. flesh   (d) kind of color

_____ 5. grinding up   (e) soft parts of the body, not bones

Write about it.

1. Write two sentences about the same subject (write about a different subject from the selection). Use one of the words from "Match the words with their meanings."

2. There are many stories about bears, such as "Goldilocks and the Three Bears." Write your own bear story. It can be a made-up story (fiction) or about real bears (nonfiction).

12   A Fishy Story

Can a fish live out of water?

Have you ever seen a fish walking along the street? You might if you lived in Florida. This is where the "walking catfish" lives, and it really can walk! It pushes itself along with its front **fins**. Each fin has a **stiff spine**. The spines dig into the ground and help the fish move along.

But how does the walking catfish live out of the water? It is able to because it can breathe both in and out of the water. It breathes in the water with its **gills** as other fish do, but it also has things like our lungs so it can breathe out of the water, too.

The passage is about a fish that

    (a) cannot swim   (b) can live out of   (c) can talk

                          the water

Can you remember?

1. Catfish live in

    (a) Florida   (b) Boston   (c) Canada

2. How does the catfish walk? It uses its
   - (a) gills
   - (b) lungs
   - (c) fins

3. The catfish breathes in the water with its
   - (a) gills
   - (b) lungs
   - (c) fins

4. The catfish breathes out of the water by
   - (a) flapping its fins
   - (b) using spines that dig into the ground
   - (c) using things like our lungs

5. Which would find it easier to live if a pond dried up?
   - (a) normal fish
   - (b) the catfish
   - (c) you could not say from this passage

Put the sentences in the correct order.

_____ It's because it can breathe both in and out of the water.

_____ Each fin has a stiff spine.

_____ Have you ever seen a fish walking down the street?

_____ How can the walking catfish live out of water?

Match the words with their meanings.

_____ 1. fins   (a) hard to bend or move

_____ 2. stiff   (b) part of a fin that is stiff and pointed

_____ 3. spine   (c) part of a fish, like wings, used to steer

_____ 4. gills   (d) what fish use to breathe

Write about it.

1. Write two sentences about the same subject (write about a different subject from the selection). Use one of the words from "Match the words with their meanings."

2. Imagine that you are a reporter for a Florida newspaper. Write about a day when the walking catfish came to your town. Write the facts you have learned from this selection about the walking catfish and tell what some townspeople said when they saw the fish walking down the street.

13 Moving Twice a Year

What animal moves its house every six months?

As soon as it begins to get cold in the fall you can hear a **bustle** and **rustle** in the trees and **honking** and splashing in lakes. It happens every year. The noise comes from **flocks** of birds getting ready for their trip south.

Some birds, like the snow goose, fly in a V-shape, high in the sky. They always go the same way to the same place. Snow geese travel thousands of miles to their winter homes. No one knows how they find their way.

Then in the spring they make the trip back again — to the same homes they used the summer before.

Not all birds make it. They may run into bad weather, wild animals, or hunters. Some crash into tall buildings, telephone poles, or even window panes.

The passage is about

    (a) birds nesting   (b) how birds change   (c) keeping birds
                                   their homes   as pets

Can you remember?

1. Birds get ready for their trip south in the
    (a) summer   (b) fall   (c) winter

2. What shape do snow geese fly in?
    (a) Y   (b) V   (c) X

3. They don't
    (a) go the same way   (b) go to the same   (c) get lost
                                   place

4. Which of these may be harmful to the birds?
    (a) flowers   (b) trees   (c) TV antennas

5. The birds fly north in the
    (a) spring   (b) summer   (c) fall

Put the sentences in the correct order.

_____ In the spring the geese make the trip back again.

_____ It takes place every year.

_____ Not all the birds make it.

_____ Snow geese travel thousands of miles.

Match the words with their meanings.

_____ 1. bustle   (a) a loud, sharp noise made by birds

_____ 2. rustle   (b) lots of little sounds, like the moving of dry

_____ 3. flocks   leaves

_____ 4. honking   (c) groups of animals living and traveling
                             together

                        (d) moving around with lots of noise; in a rush

Write about it.

1. Write two sentences about the same subject (write about a different subject from the selection). Use one of the words from "Match the words with their meanings."

2. The snow goose and many other birds have summer and winter homes. Would you like to change homes twice a year or stay in the same place always? Explain your choice.

14 Clouds

Can you tell what this poem is about?

White sheep, white sheep
On a blue hill,
When the wind stops
You all stand still.

When the wind blows
You walk away slow.
White sheep, white sheep
Where do you go?

—Christina Rossetti

The poem is about

  (a) sheep   (b) clouds   (c) hills

Can you remember?

1. The hill was

  (a) brown   (b) green   (c) blue

2. The hill really is

  (a) a mountain   (b) the sky   (c) the sea

3. When the wind stops they all
    (a) stand still   (b) blow away   (c) change shape
4. When the wind blows they
    (a) go fast   (b) go away   (c) fall
5. The poet wants to know
    (a) where they came   (b) where they are   (c) what they are
        from   going

What do you notice about this poem?

1. Which words rhyme? List them.

_____

2. How many verses are there?

_____

3. Where do you look for the writer's name?

_____

4. Which line can be read in both verses?

_____

Write about it.

1. Write two sentences about the same subject (write about a different subject from the selection). Use one of the words from "Match the words with their meanings."

2. Write a poem about something else in nature, such as rain, sun, or wind. Choose words to describe this part of nature—tell what it looks, sounds, or feels like.

15 Mr. Nobody

Who is Mr. Nobody?

I know a funny little man,
  As quiet as a mouse,
Who does the **mischief** that is done
  In everybody's house!
There's no one ever sees his face,
  And yet we all **agree**,
That every plate we break was cracked
  By Mr. Nobody.
'Tis he who always tears our books,
  Who leaves the door **ajar**.
He pulls the buttons from our shirts,
  And **scatters** pins afar.
That squeaking door will always squeak,
  For **prithee**, don't you see,
We leave the oiling to be done
  By Mr. Nobody.

  —Anonymous

The poem is about

(a) a small man (b) a mouse (c) someone we blame for our mistakes or carelessness

Can you remember?

1. Mr. Nobody
   (a) is noisy (b) is quiet (c) likes to sing

2. We blame Mr. Nobody for
   (a) broken cups (b) cracked plates (c) lost books

3. We lose
   (a) our books (b) buttons from our shirts (c) our shoes

4. We don't
   (a) put our books away (b) close the door (c) make our beds

5. Mr. Nobody works
   (a) during the day (b) at night (c) it doesn't say

Put the sentences in the correct order.

_____ 'Tis he who always tears our books,

_____ I know a funny little man,

_____ There's no one ever sees his face,

_____ That squeaking door will always squeak,

Match the words with their meanings.

_____ 1. agree   (a) partly open

_____ 2. mischief   (b) harm, damage

_____ 3. ajar   (c) feel the same way about

_____ 4. scatters   (d) pray thee — an old-fashioned word

_____ 5. prithee   (e) spreads out

Write about it.

1. Write two sentences about the same subject (write about a different subject from the selection). Use one of the words from "Match the words with their meanings."

2. Imagine that you review poems for a poetry magazine. Write your opinion of "Mr. Nobody." Be sure to give the reasons for your opinion.

16 Making Brownies

Giving a party? Need a nice end to a picnic? Want a snack during the day? Here's a quick and easy way to make good brownies.

You need: 2 cups **crushed** graham crackers

1 large packet of chocolate chips

1 cup **chopped** nuts

1 cup **evaporated milk**

1. Turn the oven on to 350°.

2. Put everything into a bowl and **mix** well.

3. Rub butter on a baking sheet.

4. Spread your **mixture** evenly onto the baking sheet.

5. Put into the oven and bake for 30 minutes.

6. Let it cool for 3-5 minutes. Then cut it into squares while it's still soft.

The passage is about

    (a) giving a party   (b) eating brownies   (c) making brownies

Can you remember?

1. To make these brownies you need

    (a) sugar   (b) flour   (c) nuts

2. The milk should be

    (a) fresh   (b) sour   (c) canned

3. You mix everything

    (a) in a pan   (b) in a bowl   (c) on a baking sheet

4. You cook the brownies for

    (a) 10 minutes   (b) 20 minutes   (c) 30 minutes

5. What do you do after the brownies have been out of the oven for 3-5 minutes?

    (a) stir them   (b) crush them   (c) cut them

Put the sentences in the correct order.

_____ Evenly spread your mixture onto the baking sheet.

_____ Put the mixture into the oven.

_____ Turn the oven on to 350°.

_____ Put everything into a bowl.

Match the words with their meanings.

_____ 1. crushed   (a) cut up

_____ 2. chopped   (b) milk that has been made thicker by heating to

_____ 3. evaporated milk   take some of the water from it

_____ 4. mix   (c) everything that has been stirred together

_____ 5. mixture   (d) broken up into small bits

                     (e) stir together

Write about it.

1. Write two sentences about the same subject (write about a different subject from the selection). Use one of the words from "Match the words with their meanings."

2. Find a recipe that is easy and fun to make. Then tell what foods you need to make it and write the directions so your classmates can cook the dish.

17 A Tale of a Tail

The lizard lost its tail, but it was happy, not sad. Why?

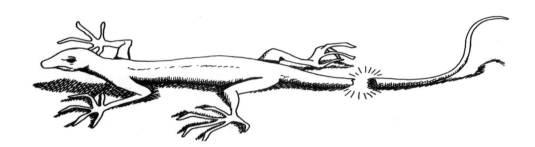

The lizard had lost its tail but it was not sad, for the lost tail had saved the lizard's life.

When an alligator (AL-i-gay-ter) lizard is **attacked** by an **enemy** it **drops** its tail. The tail has a part where the bone breaks off easily. The break closes quickly to stop the lizard from bleeding.

The tail keeps **wriggling** after it leaves the lizard's body. The attacker thinks it's still part of the lizard and **pounces** on it. This gives the lizard time to get away.

In time the lizard grows a new tail. Clever, isn't it?

The story is about

    (a) how lizards save themselves   (b) how to get a new tail   (c) why the lizard's tail wriggles

Can you remember?

1. When the lizard lost its tail it was

    (a) cross   (b) happy   (c) sad

2. When the lizard is attacked it

    (a) curls up   (b) bites   (c) drops its tail

3. Its tail is
   (a) long   (b) short   (c) it doesn't say

4. The break closes
   (a) quickly   (b) slowly   (c) it does not close

5. After the tail leaves the lizard it
   (a) does not move   (b) keeps on   (c) turns brown
                                  wriggling

Put the sentences in the correct order.

_____ The lizard lost its tail.

_____ Clever, isn't it?

_____ The alligator lizard drops its tail.

_____ The attacker thinks the tail is still part of the lizard.

Match the words with their meanings.

_____ 1. enemy   (a) twisting and moving about like a worm

_____ 2. drops   (b) lets fall

_____ 3. wriggling   (c) jumps on quickly

_____ 4. attacked   (d) fought by someone

_____ 5. pounces   (e) one who wants to harm another; opposite of friend

Write about it.

1. Write two sentences about the same subject (write about a different subject from the selection). Use one of the words from "Match the words with their meanings."

2. Do you think the alligator lizard has any other way to fight an attacker besides dropping its tail? What would probably happen to the lizard if it were unable to drop its tail? Write your opinion and give the reasons for your belief.

18 Time

Here's a new way to remember time.

How many seconds in a minute?
Sixty, and no more in it.

How many minutes in an hour?
Sixty for sun and **shower**.

How many hours in a day?
Twenty-four for work and play.

How many days in a week?
Seven, both to hear and speak.

How many weeks in a month?
Four, as the **swift** moon runn'th.

How many months in a year?
Twelve, the **almanac** makes clear.

How many years in an **age**?
Many, many, says the **sage**.

How many ages in time?
No one knows the rhyme.

—Christina Rossetti

The poem is about

    (a) how to tell the time
    (b) the way we measure time
    (c) how old the world is

Can you remember?

1. How many seconds are there in a minute?

    (a) 6   (b) 16   (c) 60

2. How many minutes are there in an hour?

    (a) 6   (b) 16   (c) 60

3. How many hours are there in a day?

    (a) 6   (b) 12   (c) 24

4. How many months are there in a year?

    (a) 6   (b) 12   (c) 24

5. What does the last verse mean?

    (a) life will go on forever
    (b) we cannot measure how long life will go on
    (c) it's hard to make up poems

Put the sentences in the correct order.

_____ How many years in an age?

_____ How many weeks in a month?

_____ How many days in a week?

_____ How many minutes in an hour?

Match the words with their meanings.

_____ 1. shower   (a) wise person

_____ 2. swift   (b) a long time

_____ 3. almanac   (c) rain

_____ 4. (an) age   (d) fast, quick

_____ 5. sage   (e) calendar

Write about it.

1. Write two sentences about the same subject (write about a different subject from the selection). Use one of the words from "Match the words with their meanings."

2. People often complain that time goes too quickly or too slowly. ("Time flies when you're having fun!" or "This day is dragging on and on.") Write a story about a day when time isn't passing as quickly or slowly as you would like. You can make up a story or write about a real day.

19 Going on a Camping Trip

Carla was going on a **camping** trip. What did she take?

Carla was **excited** because she was going on a camping trip. She had all her things ready and was now going to pack them in her **knapsack**.

On her bed she had put all the clothes she would need: 4 pairs of socks; 6 pants; 1 pair of jeans; 2 sweaters; 2 shorts.

On the table she had put the food: 3 cans of meat; 2 cans of tuna fish; 4 cans of soup; 8 cookies in a packet; 6 candy bars.

On the floor she had put things she would need to eat with: 1 **mug**; 2 plates; 1 pan; 3 spoons; 2 knives; 2 forks.

Do you think she got everything into her knapsack? You may go back and read the passage as you answer the questions.

The passage is about

   (a) packing for a
       camping trip

   (b) how to cook on
       a camping trip

   (c) what you can get
       into a knapsack

Can you remember?

1. How many pairs of jeans did Carla take?
      (a) 5   (b) 1   (c) 3

2. How many cans of food did she take?
      (a) 5   (b) 9   (c) 12

3. If you add the cookies and candy bars there are
      (a) 12   (b) 14   (c) 16

4. How many things did she take to eat with?
      (a) 10   (b) 11   (c) 12

5. What did she *not* take?
      (a) a pan   (b) a sweater   (c) a map

Put the sentences in the correct order.

_____ Carla had all her things ready.

_____ On her bed were all the clothes she would need.

_____ On the floor she had put things she would need to eat with.

_____ Carla had put the food on the table.

Match the words with their meanings.

_____ 1. excited   (a) a cloth bag you put on your back

_____ 2. camping   (b) pleased and happy

_____ 3. mug   (c) living outdoors overnight

_____ 4. knapsack   (d) large, heavy cup with a handle

Write about it.

1. Write two sentences about the same subject (write about a different subject from the selection). Use one of the words from "Match the words with their meanings."

2. Describe what you would take on a six-day camping trip in the woods. Remember that you will need to carry everything on your back.

20 A Puzzling Shape

How many **squares** are in the shape below?

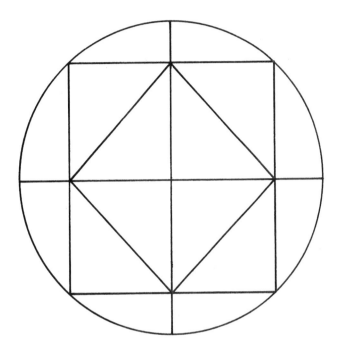

A **circle** is round like an orange. It is made up of one **curved** line and forms a ring. That is why the gold circle you put on your finger is called a ring.

A square has four sides. The sides are straight; they are all the same **length**.

A **triangle** has three sides. The sides are all straight, but they need not be the same length.

The passage is about

   (a) shapes   (b) patterns   (c) drawings

Can you remember?

1. How many circles are in the shape?

   (a) 1   (b) 2   (c) 3

2. How many squares are in the shape?

   (a) 2   (b) 4   (c) 6

3. How many triangles are in the shape?

   (a) 8   (b) 12   (c) 10

4. A circle is made up of

   (a) one line   (b) two lines   (c) three lines

5. A square has

   (a) two long and   (b) four sides the (c) six sides the
        two short sides   same length   same length

Put the sentences in the correct order.

_____ A triangle has three sides.

_____ A square has four sides.

_____ A circle forms a ring.

_____ A circle is round like an orange.

Match the words with their meanings.

_____ 1. square   (a) completely round shape

_____ 2. circle   (b) bent; not straight

_____ 3. curved   (c) how long something is

_____ 4. length   (d) three-sided shape

_____ 5. triangle   (e) a shape with four sides the same length

Write about it.

1. Write two sentences about the same subject (write about a different subject from the selection). Use one of the words from "Match the words with their meanings."

2. Draw your own puzzling shape. Use circles, squares, rectangles, triangles, or other shapes. Then tell how many of each shape there are in your drawing.

21 The Camel's Hump

How did the camel get its **hump**?

There once was a camel who was very **lazy**. It sat in the sun and ate while all the other camels worked hard carrying heavy loads across the desert.

"Come and help us. Then we need not carry so much," called the other camels. But the lazy camel only **laughed**. It wasn't going to get tired carrying those heavy loads.

One day a young girl came by with a large **jug** of water. She was hot and so tired she could not go one more step.

"Kind camel," she said, "You are strong. Please help me. My father is very sick and I must get this water to him before tonight."

"I'm far too busy," said the camel. It **yawned** and took another snack.

"You are lazy and good for nothing," cried the girl. Suddenly she turned into the witch she really was. "Because you are so lazy you will always carry a load on your back."

And from that day the camel has had a hump on its back.

The story is about

    (a) a lazy witch   (b) a lazy girl   (c) a lazy camel

Can you remember?

1. The camel liked to

    (a) play   (b) eat   (c) talk

2. The other camels

    (a) sat in the sun   (b) talked to each   (c) carried heavy loads
                                   other

3. The young girl had

    (a) water   (b) a jug   (c) a bag

4. Her sick father needed

    (a) water   (b) milk   (c) food

5. How did the camel get its hump?

    (a) it was born with it   (b) by eating too   (c) it was given it
                                   much   by a witch

Put the sentences in the correct order.

_____ There was a camel who was very lazy.

_____ One day a young girl walked by.

_____ "Come and help us."

_____ Ever since then the camel has had a hump on its back.

Match the words with their meanings.

_____ 1. lazy   (a) opened the mouth wide

_____ 2. laughed   (b) not wanting to work

_____ 3. jug   (c) a lump, usually on the back

_____ 4. hump   (d) made sounds that show one thinks something is

_____ 5. yawned   funny or silly

                      (e) something to put liquid in, usually made of
                           pottery

Write about it.

1. Write two sentences about the same subject (write about a different subject from the selection). Use one of the words from "Match the words with their meanings."

2. Write your own story telling how the camel got its hump.

22 Have You Ever Seen the Wind?

Who has seen the wind?
   Neither I nor you:
But when the leaves hang **trembling**,
   The wind is **passing through**.
Who has seen the wind?
   Neither you nor I:
But when the trees **bow** down their heads,
   The wind is passing by.

—Christina Rossetti

54

The poem is about

    (a) why everyone can   (b) how no one can   (c) why the wind
        see the wind   see the wind   blows hard in winter

Can you remember?

1. The wind does *not* make

    (a) the leaves tremble   (b) the trees bow   (c) the trees unhappy
                     their heads

2. "Neither I nor you" means

    (a) not everyone   (b) not some people   (c) not the two of us

3. The poem tells us

    (a) birds live in trees   (b) the trees are tall   (c) the wind shakes the
                                      leaves

4. "Bow down your heads" means the wind

    (a) breaks off the   (b) makes the trees   (c) makes the trees
        tops of the trees   bend   short

5. We can tell when there is a wind because

    (a) the leaves move   (b) the leaves   (c) the leaves die
                    change color

Put the sentences in the correct order.

_____ But when the trees bow down their heads,

_____ When the leaves hang trembling.

_____ The wind is passing through.

_____ The wind is passing by.

Match the words with their meanings.

_____ 1. neither   (a) going through, going by

_____ 2. trembling   (b) bend

_____ 3. passing through   (c) shaking

_____ 4. bow   (d) not either

Write about it.

1. Write two sentences about the same subject (write about a different subject from the selection). Use one of the words from "Match the words with their meanings."

2. Write a story about a windy day. How does the wind affect the people, animals, or things in your story?

23 The Lion and the Mouse

A mouse woke up a lion by mistake. What would you say to the lion if you were the mouse?

One day a mouse bumped into a sleeping lion and woke him up. The angry lion **snatched** up the **frightened** mouse in his paws. But before the lion could eat him the mouse cried out, "I'm sorry. I didn't mean to wake you. Please let me go and one day I will do you a **favor** in return."

The lion laughed. "What can a small mouse like you do for me, the king of the animals?" he asked. But he let the mouse go.

A week later the mouse heard the lion **roaring**. He was caught in a hunter's net. Remembering his promise, the mouse quickly **gnawed** his way through the ropes until the lion was free.

The lion now understood that size was not always the most important thing.

The story is about

   (a) a joke played on
a lion by a mouse

   (b) how a mouse
caught a lion

   (c) how a mouse
saved a lion

Can you remember?

1. The lion was
   (a) lying in the sun   (b) sleeping   (c) eating

2. The mouse said
   (a) the lion was   (b) he would never   (c) he would do the
       greedy   disturb the   lion a favor
                                 lion again

3. The lion thought the mouse was
   (a) funny   (b) brave   (c) unfriendly

4. The mouse heard the lion roaring
   (a) one day later   (b) one week later   (c) one month later

5. After being saved, the lion understood
   (a) you get what   (b) you can't do   (c) size is not
       you deserve   without a friend   always important

Put the sentences in the correct order.

_____ The lion laughed.

_____ The mouse gnawed through the rope.

_____ A mouse bumped into a sleeping lion.

_____ The lion was caught in a hunter's net.

Match the words with their meanings.

_____ 1. snatched   (a) afraid

_____ 2. frightened   (b) a loud noise, usually made in fear or anger

_____ 3. favor   (c) chewed

_____ 4. roaring   (d) a kindness, something helpful

_____ 5. gnawed   (e) grabbed

Write about it.

1. Write two sentences about the same subject (write about a different subject from the selection). Use one of the words from "Match the words with their meanings."

2. Write a story in which being small is better than being large. Your story can be about an animal or a person.

24   A Space Attack

Which space ship is this story about, No. 1 or No. 2?

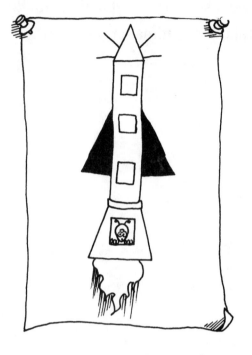

No. 1 Fred's Drawing   No. 2 Sally's Drawing

The crew of **Flight** 9 were on their usual weekly trip into outer space. They had just passed a **giant** star when they were attacked by the strangest space ship. Quickly, Captain Filco called back to earth on the radio. This is how Captain Filco **described** the space ship to Fred and Sally, who were listening to the radio.

"It is made of shining metal. It has four square windows. Out of one window an **odd** face is staring at us. The ship looks like it is made from three parts. The front is in the shape of a triangle with a pointed nose. It has four **antennas** sticking out from it. The middle is long and thin, like a tube. It has two wings. The end gets wider and has flames coming out of it."

Fred and Sally both made drawings of the space ship. Who was the better listener?

The story is about

    (a) rockets   (b) space ships   (c) robots

Can you remember?

1. What were they near when they were attacked?

    (a) earth   (b) a giant star   (c) Mars

2. How many parts made up the body of the space ship?

    (a) 1   (b) 2   (c) 3

3. Which shape were the windows?

    (a) △   (b) □   (c) ○

4. One of the drawings does not have

    (a) four square   (b) four antennas   (c) flames
        windows

5. Which space ship is this story about?

    (a) No. 1   (b) No. 2   (c) neither of them

Put the sentences in the correct order.

_____ Fred and Sally both drew pictures.

_____ The crew of Flight 9 were on their usual weekly trip.

_____ It is made of shining metal.

_____ Captain Filco quickly called back to earth base.

Match the words with their meanings.

_____ 1. flight   (a) told about

_____ 2. described   (b) very big, huge

_____ 3. giant   (c) moveable feelers on the heads of insects,

_____ 4. odd   spiders, lobsters, and crabs.

_____ 5. antennas   (d) trip in the air made by an airplane or space
                     ship (or a bird)

                    (e) strange, unusual

Write about it.

1. Write two sentences about the same subject (write about a different subject from the selection). Use one of the words from "Match the words with their meanings."

2. Draw your own space ship. Then describe it, using lots of details.

25 Strange Footprints

How many words meaning "big" can you find in the story?

Tom and the other campers had been climbing up the **steep** mountain **slope** for some time when they suddenly came upon the enormous footprints.

Tom stopped and stared in **amazement**. They were over a **yard** wide and as long as he was tall. Tom pointed them out to his friends. "They must belong to some **colossal** animal," he cried, for there were large spaces between each footprint. They were also deep, showing that the animal not only had very long legs but was very heavy, too.

"I have never seen such gigantic footprints," said Jenny. "They must belong to Big Foot." They never did find out what had made the enormous footprints because it soon became dark and they had to return to home.

The story is about

　　(a) a mountain lion　　　(b) Big Foot　　　(c) some large footprints

Do you remember?

1. How many campers were there?

   (a) 6   (b) 9   (c) it does not say

2. The footprints were

   (a) a yard wide   (b) over a yard wide   (c) less than a yard wide

3. The footprints were as long as the height of

   (a) a child   (b) an adult   (c) a house

4. The footprints were

   (a) close together   (b) far apart   (c) in pairs

5. The campers never found out to whom the footprints belonged because

   (a) they were afraid   (b) they got lost   (c) they had to
                                                        return home

Put the sentences in the correct order.

_____ It soon became dark.

_____ "They must belong to some colossal animal," he cried.

_____ He stopped and stared in amazement.

_____ "I have never seen such gigantic footprints," said Jenny.

Match the words with their meanings.

_____ 1. slope   (a) great surprise

_____ 2. amazement   (b) gigantic, huge

_____ 3. yard   (c) land that is slanting, not flat

_____ 4. colossal   (d) about three feet in length

_____ 5. steep   (e) getting very high very quickly

Write about it.

1. Write two sentences about the same subject (write about a different subject from the selection). Use one of the words from "Match the words with their meanings."

2. There are many stories about giant creatures such as Big Foot. Write your own story about a giant animal or person. If you wish, read some other stories about giants and compare those stories to yours.

26   Phillis Wheatley

Who was Phillis Wheatley?

How would you like to be taken **suddenly** from your home and country? That is what happened to Phillis Wheatley when she was only eight years old. In 1761 she was taken from Africa to Boston, where she became a **slave**.

But Phillis was lucky. The Wheatleys, the family who took her, were kind. They treated her well. They even taught her to read and write, which was very unusual.

Phillis was excited when she could write. Now she could write down all the things that had been going through her mind. She began to write poems. At the end of her life, Phillis Wheatley lived alone, a free woman, and continued to write poetry. Her poems were so good people still read them today.

The passage is about

   (a) a painter   (b) a **poet**   (c) an actress

Can you remember?

1. How old was Phillis when she was taken from her home?

   (a) 4   (b) 8   (c) 10

2. Where was her home?

    (a) Africa   (b) China   (c) Mexico

3. Where was she taken to?

    (a) Washington   (b) Boston   (c) Los Angeles

4. What excited Phillis?

    (a) learning to read   (b) learning to write   (c) being set free

5. Where did Phillis get her last name?

    (a) she was given   (b) she took it from   (c) it was where she
       it by her parents   the family she   lived
                            lived with

Put the sentences in the correct order.

_____ She began to write poems.

_____ Phillis was lucky.

_____ The Wheatleys treated her well.

_____ How would you like to be suddenly taken from your home and country?

Match the words with their meanings.

_____ 1. suddenly   (a) person who writes poems

_____ 2. slave   (b) all at once, without expecting it

_____ 3. poet   (c) someone who is owned by another person
                            and must do whatever that person wants

Write about it.

1. Write two sentences about the same subject (write about a different subject from the selection). Use one of the words from "Match the words with their meanings."

2. Phillis Wheatley was glad to learn to write so she could write down what she'd been thinking. Write two or three paragraphs that express what you think about something. Some examples: your favorite animal and why you like it, whether parents should let kids eat whatever they want, what bedtime you would like and why.

27 How to Make a Sand Picture

Have you ever made a sand picture?

I have a pretty **paperweight** that has a sand picture of the desert and mountains. It was made by a Native American. Native Americans have been making sand pictures for thousands of years. And you can too.

All you need is: a dry glass jar; some spoons; a paintbrush; some different colored sand (found in supermarkets, hardware stores, and variety stores); and a **steady** hand. A wrong move of the hand may spoil your picture.

Start by making this simple **pattern**. Later you can try pictures.
1. Pour the first layer of sand into the jar. Then add more layers of different colored sands. Use your paintbrush to make the layers **level** (see picture 1).
2. Press the tip of the paintbrush **handle** against the inside of the jar and push it down. The sand will move down, too, and make your pattern (see picture 2).

The passage is about

    (a) painting a picture
    (b) making a sand picture
    (c) making a picture on glass

Can you remember?

1. Who made the first sand pictures?
    (a) early American settlers
    (b) Native Americans
    (c) they were not made until today

2. What you do not need in order to make a sand picture is
   (a) water   (b) a paint brush   (c) a jar

3. What may spoil your picture?
   (a) a wrong move   (b) too much paint   (c) too much sand

4. You make the layers even by
   (a) using a paintbrush   (b) poking in your   (c) shaking the jar
                                finger

5. You make the pattern by
   (a) pressing the   (b) putting in more   (c) shaking the jar
       paintbrush down   sand

Put the sentences in the correct order.

_____ Next add more layers of different colored sands.

_____ Press the end of the paintbrush handle against the inside of the jar.

_____ The sand that is pushed down makes a pattern.

_____ Pour the first layer of sand into the jar.

Match the words with their meanings.

_____ 1. paperweight   (a) something small and heavy to hold down
_____ 2. steady   papers on a desk
_____ 3. pattern   (b) lines and shapes that make a design
_____ 4. level   (c) no bumps; flat, even
_____ 5. handle   (d) the part you hold onto
                            (e) firm and still, not shaky

Write about it.

1. Write two sentences about the same subject (write about a different subject from the selection). Use one of the words from "Match the words with their meanings."

2. Making sand pictures is fun. Describe something you like to make, such as an art project or a recipe, and explain how you make it. Be sure to mention everything you need to make it.